Esquire's

THINGS
A MAN
SHOULD
KNOW

Esquire's

THINGS
A MAN
SHOULD
KNOW

SEX about

HEARST BOOKS
NEW YORK

Library of Congress Cataloging-in-Publication Data
Omelianuk, Scott.
    Esquire's things a man should know about sex / Scott Omelianuk, Ted Allen.
        p. cm.

    ISBN 1-58816-029-7
    1. Sex instruction for men. I. Title: Things a man should know about sex. II. Allen, Ted.
    III. Esquire (New York, N.Y.) IV. Title.

    HQ36 .O47 2001
    306.7'081—dc21

                                                                    00-063208

DESIGN BY SERG ANDREYEV, NEUWIRTH & ASSOCIATES, INC.
COVER DESIGN BY TODD ALBERTSON
COVER PHOTOGRAPHS BY FABRIZIO FERRI © 2000.

First Edition
1 2 3 4 5 6 7 8 9 10

Printed in Mexico
www.esquire.com

Introduction

You know, of course, that you want it. Among
the many lessons we are taught from birth—
before birth, really, what with genes and
instinct and all—none is clearer than this: We
will spend our lives wanting it. Not merely
wanting, of course: craving it, savoring it, sali-
vating at the merest glimmer of the idea of it,
verily, by definition, *lusting*. We read books
and watch movies and witness the behavior of
sultry waitresses and randy single uncles, and
one thing we learn for sure is that we must do
anything, anything at all—risk prison, jettison
friends, beg, shoplift, embezzle, scream, listen
to Enya, beg, get religion, change religions,
trash careers, shoot hand-tooled shotguns into

the starry Indonesian sky, beg, crash the Porsche, sky-dive, seek counseling, borrow, beg, align chakras, drink poison, beg, kill, kill again, be killed, rise from the dead, and most especially, having little recourse remaining, beg—if there is even the slimmest chance that it might result in a little bit of netherly friction, which is to say, sex.

What most men don't know, unfortunately, is how to do it.

Oh, we might think we do, but the writers and researchers of this volume have it on good authority (women) that many of us (men) don't. Even if not one of us (men) will admit it.

We are not taught Word One about performing things sexual, even now, when concerns about polite conversation seem ridiculously quaint. In particular, we men are never schooled in the sorts of things sexual that *women* might enjoy—an important consideration, that, at least among those seeking your more common sexual arrangement of one male and one female. Indeed, who would tell us such things? Dad? Er, *Mom?* Professionally trained and certified health teachers in the primary grades, who all seem to be overweight gym teachers in stretchy pants whose last erection quite possibly occurred on a weekend furlough during the Korean War? Even if these people were willing and able, are they really the ones from whom we'd choose to learn the finer points of, say, toe nibbling?

No. Rather, that would be us. Not in person, of course. But in print, in this book, here.

We have talked to the womenfolk. They have told us many things that you should know. We also have consulted important studies of human sexual behavior, from the classics (Hite, Kinsey, Erica Jong, Snoop Dogg) to the groundbreaking University of Chicago report of 1996, except where we made things up completely. We have argued and debated and arrived at conclusions. We have culled fascinating statistics and lore, because everybody wants to measure himself (sometimes literally) against his peers. And we have tried throughout to keep our sense of humor—because if there's one thing sex should nearly always involve, it is not only warmth and fondness, if not love, but the acceptance of laughter—though never at that moment when your trousers drop.

As they say, birds do it. Bees do it. Even so-and-so's in the trees do it. But how about this: Let us do it (not you and us, but us in a more general sense, of course). Yes, let's do it, but let's do it really, really well.

CHAPTER one:

WHEREIN WE ARE reminded, and reminded once more, and then a third time, emphatically, that when one is having sex with a woman, it is advisable to arrange the experience such that she, too, will feel as if she is having sex. Plus: sex in the office.

It's about her.

Except when it's about her.

Which is to say that by far the most crucially important thing to know, and to remember at all times, for the rest of your functionally pneumatic life (and afterward, too): Your primary objective is to make her very, very happy.

Because it is easy to make yourself happy. You can do that all by yourself—even with one hand tied behind your back.

Now, then: Begin at the neck.

Slowly.

And you know how when you're there, at the neck, you often make that move for the inside of her ear with your tongue? Don't do that.

Because, besides being a vector for some kind of inner-ear infection, a wet willie administered directly with the tongue is an acquired taste that very few people acquire.

See, sex is one of those things in which everything you need to know you did not learn in kindergarten.

Or in high school.

Especially not in high school.

News from the womenfolk: They want you to know that female sexuality involves regions other than the obvious naughty bits.

Further, what appeals to one woman doesn't necessarily appeal to the next.

An example, and one that might come as a shock: Some women think that too much time spent on the bazooms can become unpleasant and slightly, disturbingly Oedipal.

What appeals to no woman: premature, shall we say, resolution. Yours.

Extra Bonus Mental Picture that might assist in the avoidance of premature resolution: Dick Cheney.

Also: Dick Cheney In jackboots and pasties and nothing else.

Whatever you do, don't try thinking about nuns—that just makes matters worse.

If rushing is simply unavoidable, know that you will be expected to last longer, much longer, in round two.

On the notion that good girls don't: Yes, they do.

Surefire signs that she wants to take you to bed: There are no surefire signs that she wants to take you to bed.

Good signs that she's considering it: laughs at your jokes, smiles most of the time, occasionally gently contradicts you (to show she cares enough to engage you and is confident enough to disagree), touches you softly every now and again.

Handing you her panties under the table at the restaurant might mean something too.

Good signs that she's not considering it: She doesn't laugh at your jokes, doesn't smile, contradicts you too much and with vigor, shakes your hand, and leaves the building.

Appropriate euphemism for womanly bits: Snoopy.

Also: Hoosie.

Also: What's-it.

Also: Down There.

Appropriate euphemism for manly bits: Kong.

Yeah, well, it's better than Mr. Winky.

Euphemisms for sexy bits are essential because, for some unfortunate reason, the actual medical and/or scientific words for every single one of these body parts are less than musical.

And the nonmedical and/or nonscientific ones are for hunting trips more so than books.

In addition to hunting trips, blue language can also be effective when writing a *Penthouse* letter or when judiciously applied during the act (more on which later).

Never write a letter to *Penthouse*.

News from the womenfolk: You can never, ever, under any circumstances, no matter how florid or excessive you might think you sound, exaggerate the splendor of a woman's recently unclothed body.

Caveat based on further analysis of previous item: Complimenting her naked body could easily veer into a more specific analysis of same, which could present a very dangerous situation.

Example: "Yeah, my jubblies are okay, but my what's-it is fat, don't you think?"

If such a situation is presented, be warned: Not only is EVERY SINGLE SOLITARY MOLECULE of her physical form absolutely perfect, including and perhaps most especially the what's-it in question, but you must be able to telegraph the idea that you really and truly believe this to be the gospel truth.

Alternative response in such a situation: Make like the wind, and blow; slip out the back, Jack; bad, bad scene.

You may be able to avoid this whole brouhaha if, before complimenting her naked body, you often compliment her clothed body.

More on the language of love. Menage à trois: French for "In your dreams."

Back-Door Action: See previous item.

Shrimping: Toe-sucking.

Felching: Do not ask.

Never use the word "intercourse."

Never use the word "coitus."

**Exception: Use of the word "coitus" is permissible if
you are a professional hip-hop artist and you need
something that rhymes with "annoyed us."**

Never use the word "whoopee."

Because anyone who would consider using the word "whoopee," including Bob Eubanks, is probably no longer making it.

Extra Bonus Mental Picture: Bob Eubanks, at one time or another in his life, has probably made whoopee.

Likewise, never use the word "lover."

Because it hasn't been 1973 since, jeez, 1973.

Likewise, never use the phrase "make love."

Because however verily you have torn off her bodice and no matter how rampant the state of your manroot, life is not a romance novel.

Use the word "manroot" whenever possible.

That was a joke.

When calling out your lover's name during sex, you want to be sure that it is your lover with whom you're having sex.

The authors of this book are permitted to use the term "lover" on occasion.

Because we are published authorities on sexuality, that's why.

The pet name Hugh Hefner employs in re his lover at any given moment: "My Special Lady."

Hef is in his 70s.

Plus: he's Hef.

Plus: The last time we checked, he had four "special ladies."

Cameras and sex: Not unless you're handsomely paid.

And handsome.

Video cameras and sex: Hey, it's your speedboat, Tommy Lee.

Speaking of speedboats: Know that sex is not a race.

Nor is it an endurance contest.

Yes, it is.

But only up to a point—her point, mostly.

On the other hand, sex can be looked at as a game, though not as a competition.

Sort of like tennis, when you're just hitting around.

Only no hitting.

If you *are* keeping score, and you find yourself in the lead, let her catch up.

Then, let her win.

If you win more often than you lose, then you, sir, will find yourself on the free-agent market real soon.

News from the womenfolk: It can be taken as a general article of faith that, at any given time, more than likely she is not done.

Which means you aren't either.

Anything that gets her in the mood is foreplay. Even talking. Even shopping. Even, the twisted little minx, The McLaughlin Group.

Playing Barry White, while possibly effective, is a bit transparent. Likewise Roxy Music. Try middle-period Van Morrison.

Under no circumstances shall sexual congress be attempted while playing They Might Be Giants.

Plying her with two or six zombies, while possibly effective, is wrong with a capital Wrong.

Plying her atop the boss's desk: Everybody should do this at least once.

In re sleeping your way to the top: Reconsider sleeping your way to the top.

Because it's actually much less difficult, let alone dangerous, to attain the top by working really hard.

When to sleep your way to the top: When your sultry, leggy, whip-crackin' dominatrix of a boss will settle for nothing less.

Note about aforementioned situation: Under such circumstances, it is really, really, *really* about her.

Even when it involves only a lateral move, as opposed to the top, interoffice "sleeping" is extremely risky.

Though riskiness is, in its own special way, sexy.

Note: Some companies' personnel departments now demand that interoffice romances be fully disclosed to them.

Those personnel people are a bored and horny lot, we're thinking.

What to do when the office party results in entanglement between you and a coworker: Ascertain who else knows, calculate your respective levels of regret over the situation, if applicable; slip out of the broom closet as discreetly as possible and skulk away in separate directions, never to acknowledge the incident again.

It's best to go slower than you want to, especially on first and third dates.

Because on the first date too fast will make her nervous and on the third date too slow will drive her crazy. In that good way.

Now then, frequent, fleeting touches of her arm, hand, back: Yes, do that.

Some women may find your inexperience charming.

Inexperience is more charming when coupled with an earnest willingness to learn.

Her inexperience may be charming as well.

Particularly when it's coupled with one of those Catholic-schoolgirl uniforms.

Hey! Who slipped that into the book?

News from the womenfolk: Many appreciate it when sex acts are preceded by acts of affection.

Women also want you to bring them a flower now and then. One flower is fine.

Women want you to leave them little love notes.

If and when you leave little love notes for women, they will leave little love notes for you.

Women want you to kiss them—really kiss them—more often than you do.

When kissing: Your eyes are closed.

When kissing: Your mouth is closed, initially.

When kissing: Your tongue should behave neither like a cold, dead, and gutted grouper lying on a fishmonger's ice block, nor should it tag at her tonsils like you're working the speed bag.

She's also disinclined to enjoy having her entire face slathered with saliva, for some reason.

Slathering elsewhere may be okay.

News from the womenfolk: They want you to hold their face in your hands during kisses.

A general principle as regards your tongue and its use with a woman—and this comes from a woman: on the woman, more so than in the woman.

The aforementioned tongue-guidance principle should be referenced in conjunction with the aforementioned ear and any of various other places that exist on your typical woman.

Should you fail to heed the above advice, she will consider you sloppy and will convey that opinion to her friends and will never date you again.

And neither will her friends.

Or their friends.

Because you will be officially tarred a Sloppy Kisser.

Sloppy Kissers are unpopular.

When it's good to hear laughter: When you're tickling someone.

When it's not good to hear laughter: Upon your disrobing.

How to remove a bra (from someone else, generally): Grasp either side of the clasp, and push the sides together, which should cause the hook to disengage from the eye.

Some guys can do this with one hand.

These are the same guys who, when faced with a frontal clasp, don't panic but quickly adjust.

If you are not one of these guys, don't fret. This is not a test of your manhood; you can ask her for help.

In fact, this is one of those activities, much like cooking and roller-skating, where ineptitude can actually appear "cute."

Alternatively, you could take one of Mommy's bras to practice on.

Um, hold it: No, you couldn't.

Wear no underwear emblazoned with boastful or otherwise humorous exhortations.

Like, say, Home of the Whopper.

Even if it is.

Which it isn't, most likely.

Unless it is, in which case, whoa.

When sex is in the offing, never wear briefs.

You should wear SOME type of underwear—just not briefs.

Because briefs are what little boys wear.

And they are not the most handsome garment.

Why briefs are not the most handsome garment: Their construction generally features support-related strapping that looks as if it were designed by the medical community, and that causes them to resemble a truss—and that's what old, feeble men wear.

Briefs are, in fact, a close cousin to the truss.

We don't know what a truss is, either, but we fear that we someday will.

You look better in boxers than you look naked.

She might look good in a g-string. You don't.

If you look good naked, do it with the lights on.

As long as she, too, looks good naked.

If she looks good naked, but you don't, do it with the lights on, anyway—after hiding her corrective eyewear.

Or use candlelight.

Either way, you can't expect her to be in better shape than you.

If she is in better shape than you, consider yourself lucky, start counting the days, and be prepared for the inevitable end.

Or get thyself to the StairMaster.

Top 10 Worst Pickup Lines

10. You know, I like a girl with some meat on her.

9. Hey, can you spot me a Zovirax?

8. Here—let me wipe that for you.

7. Mmm glub glub glub heh.

6. I was thinking of going bi—but you know, with dirty pillows like yours. . .

5. Wanna touch my scar?

4. Is it just me, or are you moist too?

3. Get out of my dreams. Get into my Chevette.

2. Yo! Hey, yo!

1. I'm writing a book called Things A Man Should Know About Sex; may I ask you a few questions?

Top 10 Reasons to Turn Down A Woman's Sexual Advance

10.
 9.
 8.
 7.
 6.
 5.
 4.
 3.
 2.
 1.

CHAPTER two:

Wherein we redeem the
sullied reputation of sodomy
and offer suggestions on
performing it with excellence,
propose the decriminalization
of the oral pleasuring in those
localities where it is illegal,
and consider the relative
sexiness of the French, the
Italians, and the British.

For our money, sodomy has gotten a bad rap.

What sodomy is, in part: sex that involves the use of the mouth.

What else sodomy is: certain types of sex that do not involve the front portion of one's partner, but that other portion.

Yes, exactly.

Sodomy of the oral variety shall hereafter be known as a Slurpee.

States that persist in criminalizing slurpees: Alabama, Arizona, Florida, Idaho, Louisiana, Massachusetts, Michigan, Minnesota, Mississippi, Missouri, North Carolina, Oklahoma, South Carolina, Texas, Utah, and Virginia.

Bumper-sticker idea, yours for the taking: "When Slurpees are illegal, only outlaws will get Slurpees."

The bumptious lawmakers of Idaho in particular seem to have a disproportionate fascination with other people's sex lives.

Evidence: In Idaho, sodomy carries a penalty of five years to life.

In fact, this little book is probably illegal in Idaho.

Research shows that jazz fans, gun owners, public-television watchers, concert attendees, and those who lack confidence in the president are among the most sexually active Americans.

Catholics are more sexually active than Protestants, but neither group is as active as Jews and agnostics.

Woody Allen is a Jewish-raised, agnostic jazz fan who attends concerts, almost certainly watches public television, and has a wife young enough to be his granddaughter.

Let us not think of Woody Allen at this time.

Self-described political liberals have more sex than moderates and conservatives.

Let's think neither of Michael Kinsley nor of George Will at this time, even though those two unlikely nebbishes would make sort of an interesting couple, no?

People who smoke and drink have twice as much sex as those who do not.

Let's think, shall we, of Elizabeth Hurley.

Speaking of drink, let's remember what a certain William Shakespeare said: "It provokes the desire, but takes away the performance."

Then again, the Bard also said: "I must dance barefoot on her wedding day, and, for your love to her, lead apes in hell."

He was British.

If we may invoke Shakespeare once more, sort of: The foreplay's the thing.

Foreplay being the thing, the word "foreplay" is, of course, a misnomer.

Long before foreplay: You must meet her.

Regarding the custom of buying her a drink: You don't ask, "May I buy you a drink?"

You ask, "What are you drinking?" and then you see to it that a vessel of whatever it is she is drinking is conveyed to her.

The point at which you buy her a drink: when she's nearly but not quite finished with her current drink, and no sooner.

Because to do so sooner would make it appear that you are trying to render her intoxicated.

And to do so later would be to do so too late.

And remember: Willing is better than beautiful.

Which leads us to the subject of one-night stands: Our mothers wish us to pass along their view that these are bad.

Then again, our mothers told us all cats are gray in the dark.

One-night stands: No matter how drunk you are, it is absolutely imperative that you memorize these two things before the lights go down A: Her name. B: The color of her eyes.

Because she very well might ask you.

Do you have any idea what happens when she asks you the color of her eyes and you do not know? It is bad. Very bad.

If you don't know the color of a new Friend's eyes, for God's sake don't attempt to guess—cut your losses, plead drunkenness, admit that you forgot.

Another strategy: Tell her that her eyes are hazel or ecru or whatever and if she says, "No, they're green!" and begins sobbing, you say that hazel or ecru or whatever *is* a shade of green and bet her $50 that you're right.

This betting strategy does not work when it comes to her name.

So you've got to remember her name.

FYI: Knowing her name or the color of her eyes becomes even more important on multiple-night stands, such as in, for example, a marriage.

After the first time: Don't call from your cell on the way home. Don't call first thing the next morning. Don't e-mail her your picture.

Do call the following evening, or the morning after that. Or not at all, you bastard.

Later in this relationship: We don't mean to disappoint you, but women may have less interest in watching porn than you do, but many of them wouldn't mind you watching it.

Should you choose to employ it in your home, call it erotica, not porn.

Despite the fact that more people are comfortable with erotica these days, it's still not prudent to keep it on the coffee table.

Who the hell are we kidding with this "erotica" crap? Porn is porn is porn is porn.

The G-spot: an interior region to which some women enjoy having special attention paid, and about which some women couldn't care less.

The G-spot: named for the German gynecologist Ernst Grafenberg.

We're thinking Ernst got his share, if you know what we mean.

How to locate the G-spot: Aim for it, and then ask her if your aim is true.

That said, if you ask every step of the way, you'll begin to remind her of her gynecologist.

Which, as rewarding as a career in female reproductive medicine may sound to you, is not a good thing.

If she doesn't know or won't tell you where it is: Go straight about four inches, and aim upward, back toward yourself.

Performing oral sex when suffering from nasal congestion could conceivably result in suffocation.

Receiving it: not a problem.

The people who think they are the sexiest: The French.

The people who *are* the sexiest: The Italians.

The people who are the kinkiest, although you'd never guess it and they'd never confess it without being soundly tickled on their bumcakes: The British.

For people who have hangups about oral sex: Consider that human naughty bits are almost certainly cleaner than most of the doorknobs you've touched today.

Granted, one doesn't lick doorknobs, but still.

Hot and heavy date advice: Wash.

Wash there twice.

Give as good as you get.

Make that: better than you get.

News from the womenfolk: Some women appreciate the tactile pleasures of facial hair when your face is, shall we say, south of the border.

News from the womenfolk: Some women do not appreciate the tactile pleasures of facial hair.

Either way, there is no sufficient excuse to grow a soul patch.

Come to think of it, always shave. Your face. And only your face.

Why you should only shave your face: A) chest shaving is practiced by affected Irish step-dancers and B) shaving of any other kind of body part can be dangerous—and remarkably itchy three to five days later.

For similar scratch- and itch-related risks, sex on beaches is a flawed idea.

Also alluring but flawed: sex on airplanes, sex on 50-yard lines, sex in swimming pools, sex in old-growth redwoods (you could fall and break something that ought never break).

Average duration of intercourse among American hetero-sexual couples: 10 minutes.

Average frequency of sex among American heterosexual couples: seven times a month.

News from the womenfolk: Most of them are satisfied with the amount of sex in their lives.

Much more interesting news from the womenfolk: Not ALL of them are satisfied with the amount of sex in their lives.

It would not be news that most men would be willing to have more sex.

Time a couple is most likely to engage in sex: 10:34 P.M.

One in five adults has not had sex in the last year.

Ten out of ten Americans lie through their pea-pickin' teeth about any and every aspect of their sexual lives.

Speaking of teeth: When good people give bad oral manipulations, it's the incisors and bicuspids that are usually to blame.

One is within one's rights to remind the administrator of one of those deals: It is an organ—not a gearshift, an organ. And a delicate organ, at that.

What to do when one discovers that a string is dangling from Down There: See The Curse.

The Curse: Some women's unfortunate term for their magical monthly cycle, about which it is necessary for you to know more than you want to know.

Number One: Never call it The Curse.

In fact, you could think of this aspect of her biological functioning as a blessing; it means she's not pregnant, which, when pregnancy is not desired, is, in fact, a blessing.

Her asking you to buy her feminine-hygiene products while you're out picking up beer is not a casual favor but a test of your manhood.

Some women feel more tender during certain days of their cycle, necessitating adjustment on your part in re her golden winnebagos and other areas.

Oral sex during this period: something you might wish to discuss together.

Meanwhile, back up north: You might think it would be great if, like the French, the Americans allowed their women to run around topless.

And then you might remember that the average American weighs 40 pounds more than the average Françoise.

Viagra has allowed people who would never have been able to become porn stars to, in fact, become porn stars.

It's also allowed Bob Dole to become a TV pitchman, which totally creeps us out.

Porn stars don't have as much fun as you think they do.

Bob Dole apparently has more.

Yikes.

Younger men who don't actually need Viagra sometimes use it, too, but more for recreational purposes.

Hmmm.

Fewer than five percent of married people cheat on their spouse each year.

Sixty-seven percent of that five percent is Mick Jagger.

Our third-favorite sex joke: Woman: "Do you smoke after sex?" Man: "I don't know—I've never looked."

Percentage of men who masturbated in the past year, according to the landmark book "Sex in America:" 60.

Percentage of people who believe that figure for a second: 0.

Top 10 Mood Killers

10. Saying, "Gosh, you didn't look that fat with your clothes on."

9. The sudden issuance of your girlfriend's name.

8. The sudden issuance of the word "Mommy."

7. The sudden issuance of flatulence.

6. The sudden issuance.

5. Impotence.

4. The dog copping a sniff.

3. A toddler sobbing, "Daddy, why are you hurting Mommy?!?"

2. Hearing your mother's voice on the answering machine.

1. Picking up the phone to speak with your mother.

Top 10 Bedroom Faux Pas

10. Wearing black socks.

9. Wearing pink underwear.

8. Less-than-scrupulous hygiene (exception: special-interest groups that enjoy less-than-scrupulous hygiene).

7. The biting, spanking, or inserting of anything without clearance from the tower.

6. The pushing down on the back of the head.

5. The manipulating of certain twin parts of her anatomy as one would tune a radio.

4. Covert videotaping.

3. Limiting sexual activity solely to the bedroom.

2. Excessive silence.

1. Yodeling.

CHAPTER three:

Wherein we explore the
issues of size and flavor,
the wonders of a
Brazilian bikini waxing,
and faking the male orgasm
(Oh, yes you can!!!).

Size, we've heard, doesn't matter.

Ha!

Well, not enough to justify surgery.

Surgery: For God's sake, man, that involves knives!

Surgery also requires attending nurses, who will indulge in all manner of jokes and giggling during the procedure.

As long as we're on the subject of genital mutilation: no piercings.

Because it would hurt you, and because it would creep her out.

And if it wouldn't creep her out, that's probably because she has a carriage bolt stuck someplace where it oughtn't be.

Average size, in task-oriented mode: 11 inches.

Scared you, didn't we?

True average size, in task-oriented mode: about six inches.

On the worthiness of averages, generally: The average human has one breast and half a penis, if you get our meaning.

More important than size: fit. As in, does it?

If it does not fit, you freak bastard, you might explore options other than intercourse.

Or, perhaps, consider a larger mammal.

(It is not our place to judge you.)

Men who profess small endowment are even less trustworthy than those who boast of prodigiousness.

Because anyone so fearful of prospective taunting that he's compelled to preempt it possesses a profound and potentially dangerous insecurity.

No, we are *not* obsessed with size, really, truly — this last section on the subject was no more than 50 items long.

Nonetheless, a final word: Elephant runs into a naked man on the street. Elephant looks him up and down. Elephant says: "How do you eat with that thing?"

"Blow" is just a figure of speech.

"Job," as in difficult and possibly undesirable labor, at least according to some women of our acquaintance, is decidedly not a figure of speech.

As pertains to spitting versus swallowing: Those who prefer the former—and they're well within their rights—might consider simply removing their mouths and employing a hand before this becomes an issue, so to speak.

Because spitting has distinct overtones of rejection that a hand-driven finale lacks.

In re spitting for "dietary" reasons: the caloric intake we're talking here is miniscule and would be negated with adequate exertion.

That was a joke, though you can't blame a guy for trying.

Spitting vs. swallowing, continued: it's 10 to 40 calories.

And not more than a teaspoon or so in volume.

No, ladies, we do not know why a teaspoon sometimes seems like a cup.

Foods that make for a tastier oral-sex experience: pasta, potatoes, other bland items.

Foods that do not: curry, coffee, beer, spicy items.

Recipe, it then follows, for a Slurpee-free date: chicken vindaloo washed down with a Shepherd's Tit-Bitch-Dog Ale, chased with a double espresso.

For both of your information: The above tastiness rules apply equally to men and women.

Vegetarian people taste the best.

Some people say sex is like pizza—that even when it's bad, it's still pretty good.

Some people have never slept with our ex-wife.

But seriously, folks.

Bad pizza is like bad sex: It's cold, lacks spice, and if it's really bad, the crust's too thick.

We have no idea what that means.

Bikini wax: terminology for the agonizingly painful removal of hair Down There that might otherwise poke out the sides of a swimsuit.

Brazilian wax: that variety of south-of-the-border depilation that leaves only a tiny patch just above a woman's Snoopy and removes any other trace thereof, all the way back to and including the most posterior region of all.

Yes, indeed.

Extra Bonus Mental Picture: Some people's sole source of employment income is derived from bodily yanking out hair from incredibly sensitive regions of women's bodies.

Sorry to stunt career exploration, but: Those professional bikini waxers are mostly women.

As for your predilections when it comes to the pilatory aspects of a new love, our advice would be: Take it as you find it.

Ostensibly, sex is free.

Oh, no, it isn't. No, free is one thing that sex most certainly is not.

You think you haven't paid for sex? Yes, you have.

Even if you haven't: You have. Or you will. One way or another.

Walking around you, day in and day out, are people so sexually liberated that they regularly participate in spouse-swapping, orgies, naked pool parties, and all manner of fantasy "play."

No, we don't know where to find these people, either.

What we do know: These people are why we have antibacterial soap.

Sometimes a woman will indicate she'd like to have sex (with you) and will disrobe and climb into bed and only then change her mind.

What you do when this happens: Accept it graciously.

When you accept it graciously, she'll feel more comfortable about seeing it through the next time.

We've heard that the withholding of sexual ministrations as punishment—especially ministrations involving mouths—is practiced constantly by both men and women.

Punishing by withholding sex should be stopped at once, but it won't be—so when it seems to be happening, discussion may be warranted.

What happens in the bedroom stays in the bedroom.

> Unless, of course, it happens on top of a picnic table in the Grand Tetons, or in the lox bin at Zabar's, or atop the bar in a South Detroit pool hall, or in full-Technicolor view of God and the neighbors, in which case, well, that's where it stays.

Synonym for hickey: bruise.

Bruises are not part of sex, unless you're Mickey Rourke.

To Mickey Rourke: Stop it.

Spanking is for misbehaving children.

Mostly.

Whips, ropes, and chains are for sex partners with Attention Deficit Disorder.

Mostly.

News from the womenfolk: Many women want you to play a little rougher than you do.

Because they told us, that's how we know.

It goes without saying that the extent of roughness must be discussed in advance.

This increased aggressiveness could manifest itself in the ripping off of clothes, the pinning down of arms, noisemaking, dirty talking, going faster and harder, tying wrists to bedposts, etc. —but again, you really want to discuss this in advance.

The biting of anything shall be discussed in advance.

When biting is desired, it should be known that the requesting party really means gentle biting and not the kind that could result in the removal of a protuberance.

It bears mentioning that the act of sex can result in child production.

Sex is better when nobody thinks pregnancy is likely.

Exception to the above: at such times when child production is the intent, of course.

Either way, the arrival of children often means that sex will happen less often and at lower volumes.

Hushed, infrequent sex has been known to make couples cross.

Solution: grandparents.

As babysitters, we mean, you sick bastard.

Sex is better when there's no risk of getting caught.

Excepting such times when sex is better BECAUSE there is the risk of getting caught.

News for the players of the field: Despite their drawbacks, as you know all too well, you must: condoms.

Ultra thin.

Condoms that are black or red or green or any other color that is not clear will make your manly bits appear to be black or red or green.

What you really want in a condom is this: glow-in-the-dark.

No, you don't.

We'd consider carefully the wisdom of purchasing hygiene-related potentially lifesaving products in the bathrooms of truck-stops.

Then again, they don't sell those French Ticklers just anywhere.

Most likely you need a standard-size condom.

A few of you may benefit from a slim fit one.

A fewer of you still may appreciate the larger-size condoms called, by the people at Trojan, Magnums.

How to tell what size you need, according to the dedicated staff at that purveyor of prophylactics, Condomania: Procure a cardboard toilet paper sleeve; achieve tumescence; insert that part of you which has achieved tumescence. If you fit in snugly, regular will do fine. If you swim around in there and bang from side to side a slim fit is best. If you don't fit at all: We salute you!

Which reminds us of a joke: Duck walks into a pharmacy and asks for a condom. The pharmacist says, "No problem. Shall I put it on your bill?"

News *for* the womenfolk: Men can fake orgasm, especially when wearing a condom.

Acknowledgment to the womenfolk: It is true. Men do not fake orgasm. Men are more likely to HIDE an orgasm. We're just saying: They can.

Men should participate in all birth-control decisions.

Saying "I vote for pulling out" is not adequate participation.

What you may want, if you're in a monogamous relationship and no longer desire the apparatus for conception: a vasectomy.

Realize, players of the field: The Pill stops only pregnancy, not HIV, not herpes, not any other gnarly bedbug.

Herpes, gonorrhea, syphilis, hepatitis: All of these diseases still exist.

Herpes, gonorrhea, syphilis, hepatitis: All of these diseases still exist.

Herpes, gonorrhea, syphilis, hepatitis: All of these diseases still exist, and none of those repetitions was a misprint. You're welcome.

Once more, regarding the seriousness of this: Genital herpes is just like those painful and unsightly oral cold sores, only not on your mouth, which is to say, you don't want it.

Let us now return to happy thoughts.

The woman-on-top position allows her more control over her destiny.

Some men find the woman-on-top scenario allows them more control over their duration.

The woman-on-top position does not excuse the watching of television while she does all the work.

Phone sex, such as it is: Don't use the cordless.

Because your neighbors have baby monitors, that's why.

Computer sex: Remember that nothing really gets erased from your hard drive.

Tantric sex: a yoga-related approach that involves breathing techniques and meditation and combined energies and connection with the universe, and, allegedly, hours-long sessions featuring many orgasms.

Tantric sex is a bit contrived, to our way of thinking.

Besides, there's something to be said for rolling over and passing out.

The musician Sting once said that his Tantric prowess allows him to last five hours.

Sting is full of shit.

News from the womenfolk: There are women who do not like to receive oral affections, and who wish you'd just stop it.

Not so fast: There are many more women who wish to receive oral affections every single time they have sex.

Some women who like to receive oral sex don't always want to be simultaneously performing it.

Put another way: Some women want you to know that they consider that numerically monikered act of oral coupling overrated.

One reason some women are uncomfortable receiving oral affections is their fear that men find them unpleasant Down There.

On the subject of aromas: Sexist clichés to the contrary, men and women have aromas in pretty equal measure — best get over it, say we.

On the subject of aromas: Perhaps those who don't like them just aren't cut out for sex at all, hmm?

It is perfectly acceptable to fantasize about sleeping with someone else while sleeping with the person you're actually sleeping with.

As long as that person is not, say, Dom Deluise.

Or not a person at all—a llama, for example.

Maybe it is our place to judge you, after all.

It is completely unacceptable and extraordinarily stupid to inform your partner that you're fantasizing about someone else.

In fact, many fantasies—notably those concerning furry South American fauna—are best kept to yourself.

Men and women who have been to graduate school have less sex than any other group on the educational ladder, with an average of 52 sexual acts per year.

College grads: 61 acts per year.

High school grads: 59.

Certain movements during sex, accompanied by holding the breath, can result in an inability to remember anything that occurred during intercourse for as many as 12 hours afterward.

We'd like to tell you what those movements are, but we don't remember.

People who work 60 hours or more per week are ten percent more sexually active than people who work shorter hours.

About 15 percent of adults engage in half of all sexual activity.

Eighty-seven percent of that 15 percent is Bill Clinton.

When administering a massage, warm the massage oil by rubbing it between your hands before touching the recipient.

Don't leave the massage oil on the bedside table where your friends will see it.

Leaving massage oil on the bedside table where friends can see it may generate an Extra Bonus Mental Picture of you using it.

You want to be similarly discreet with the edible panties.

Ditto any other sexual appliance, particularly anything realistic.

Speaking of which, you have no idea how many women own and utilize vibrators.

Hint: lots and lots of women.

You are not to be put off by this, even if these vibrators are large and numerous.

Although it is a bit disconcerting, isn't it, that they're all so, so unflagging?

Argument against getting a realistic looking sex toy: It will look as if it was removed from somebody.

If you're buying her a sex toy: Do not presume that she wants the biggest one—she does not.

Most likely.

Actually, you're smartest not to presume anything at all when it comes to her views on sex toys, and rather, the next time you're in the neighborhood of the appliance store, to ask her if she's interested in browsing.

Very few women achieve, shall we say, resolution solely as a result of, shall we say, intercourse.

Ways to up the chances: attending to that exterior special place—you know, the one that starts with C.

By the way, nobody actually eats the edible panties.

This just in: We're informed that some folks do, in fact, eat the edible panties.

Delightful with a '67 Chateau d'Yquem Sauternes, it turns out.

Persons who eat edible panties probably need a more serious self-help book than this one—or a good home-cooked meal.

The love doll: Deflate. Take to work. Inflate. Place in boss's chair. Skedaddle.

Name of the youthful Alabama attorney general who in 1999 actually, literally, seriously issued a ban on sex toys in the land of Lynyrd Skynyrd: Bill Pryor.

Memo to Howard Stern: Bill Pryor's phone number is (334) 242-7401.

Number of vibrators collected for shipment to the dildo-starved citizenry of Alabama by the San Francisco-based sex-toy cooperative Good Vibrations in response to the ban: 4,000.

Number of jackasses living in Alabama: at least one.

Memo to Howard Stern: The Good Vibrations phone number is (800) 289-8423.

Some leather fetishists are so passionate about their hobby as to refer to themselves in the aggregate as the "leather community."

Never use the words "leather community."

Dressing up as policemen, nurses, schoolmarms, presidents, Kentucky colonels, telephone linemen, pizza delivery boys, whatever: Knock yourself out, so long as we don't have to see it.

Sex three times a week can burn off 7,500 calories a year, the equivalent of 75 miles of running.

This does not mean that you can skip the gym.

The more sex you have, the less likely you are to suffer heart disease.

Also, the more garlic you eat, the less likely you are to suffer heart disease.

Unfortunately, the more garlic you eat, the less likely you are to have sex.

Top 10 Euphemisms for Sexual Intercourse

10. Interior decorating.

9. Parallel parking.

8. Ugandan discussions.

7. Get up in the hat rack.

6. Throw a leg over.

5. Do a bit of front-door work.

4. Let Jack in the orchard.

3. Put Barney in the VCR.

2. Take a turn among the parsley.

1. Lead the llama to the lift shaft.

Top 10 Favorite Sex Acts for Men

10. Receiving oral sex.

9. Receiving oral sex.

8. Receiving oral sex.

7. Receiving oral sex.

6. Receiving oral sex.

5. Receiving oral sex.

4. Receiving oral sex.

3. Receiving oral sex.

2. Receiving oral sex.

1. Receiving oral sex.

CHAPTER four:

Wherein we learn of Persians'
affection for soft and juicy
fruit, the exercise that will
improve sexual performance,
the perils of prematurity, and
the relative merits of the crab,
the rabbit, the wheelbarrow,
and the Cooper. Also, the
reason rough sex must always
stop when the word
"Rumplestiltskin!" is uttered.

When she says she loves your love handles, she means it.

When she says she loves your little tummy, she means it.

When she says she loves your sunken chest: Nope.

Lesbians have more sex, and longer episodes of sex, than anybody else.

Unfortunately, lesbians do not wish to have sex with you.

The Persians used to say: a woman for procreation, a young boy for pleasure, a melon for ecstasy.

You are not to follow the advice of those Persians.

Although there's certainly no harm in the occasional violation of a melon.

Our second-favorite sex joke: Man: "Do you like Kipling?" Woman: "I don't know, you naughty boy—I've never kippled."

The Chinese believe that a man derives good luck by carrying a pair of women's underwear on his person, and a woman by carrying a pair of men's.

Nowhere does this Chinese luck policy specify that the underwear needs to be *worn*.

There is an exercise that both men and women can perform to improve their sexual performance, and this exercise is called the Kegel exercise.

The Kegel exercise: repeatedly clenching the pubococcygeal muscle, better known as the muscle one tightens to stop oneself from urinating.

In men: Kegels have been shown to produce greater control over timing at the finish line, and also to improve one's ability to make one's willie dance up and down to the delight of any and all onlookers.

In women: Kegels have been shown to strengthen certain interior muscles that produce those earthshaking, mind-blowing you-know-whats — and that also gives one more control over internal squeezing/tightening motions.

One more reason to date the women of the Olympic equestrian team: The Kegel exercise happens naturally to people who ride horses.

When the moment strikes: It is not only unnecessary but actually kind of inappropriate to repeatedly holler "God!" (What are you doing, there, anyway, thanking the supreme being for this long-sought slice of sizzling action?)

However, it is better to yell "God!" than it is to yell, say, "Mommy!"

Other words best avoided during one's exertions: Pretty Mama, Hot Papa, darling daughter, cousin, auntie, grandma, Principal Skinner, Senator Kennedy, Dr. Albright, and Borgnine, you virile hunk of man, you.

Regarding threesomes: They make better fodder for naughty movies than a Saturday night out (or in, as the case may be).

Should you be so lucky threesome-wise—and don't hold your breath—everyone needs to get equal attention.

Then again, you may not want the equal attention rule to apply if it's you and another guy occupying the two-thirds majority of this particular congress.

This just in: In most cultures, high-fiving one's buddy over a woman's shoulder as one approaches, shall we say, resolution in a threesome, is considered, at a minimum, indelicate.

A sly, simple "Duuuude!" will suffice.

Jokes, folks, is what those two previous entries were, we'll thank you to realize.

We know that you give some of your best performances before breakfast, but let's everybody brush our teeth first.

Some women consider it rude for men to begin sleeping immediately after sex.

Whether they're right or wrong on this point, it's not as if cuddling is strenuous, now is it?

News from the womenfolk: Some ladies would just as soon crack a beer and turn on Speedvision as they would get all snugglykins after the fireworks.

If she rolls over and begins to snore, don't chase her for aforementioned snugglykins.

Unless you are a published authority on the subject of sexuality, you are not to use the word "snugglykins."

News from the womenfolk: The vast majority of women do *not* prefer cuddling to sex. They prefer sex.

On condoms: At the completion of one's exertions, one does not hold up the condom to inspect it.

Nor does one stretch it between thumbs and fingers like a rubber band so as to shoot it into the wastebasket.

Rather, one drops said condom discreetly onto the floor, close enough to the bed that it doesn't become a pedestrian hazard, where it can be retrieved and disposed of after an appropriate period of snug-glykins.

News from the womenfolk: Responsibility for retrieving and disposing of said prophylactic the following morning falls to—better believe it—you.

Mirrors go on walls.

Not on all four walls, please.

Beds are not round, vibrating, canopied, or filled with water.

Sheets are not satin, polyester, floral, or visibly besmirched.

Regarding sex in cars: Bear in mind the car scene from *The World According to Garp*.

Percentage of men who have received physical affection Down There from another's mouth: 79.

What we want to know is this: Who IS this sad, sorry, woebegone 21 percent, and could someone please give them a hug?

She can say no to sexual relations.

You cannot.

For many reasons, but especially because you don't want to give her the ammunition to say no the next time you want her to say yes, because you one time said no.

Speaking of which: No means no.

Except when it means yes, and it almost never means yes.

When it means yes: during consensual sexual roleplay of the mild S&M variety.

Sexual roleplay in which no means yes requires the selection of another word—a safe-word—that actually means no.

We like the word "Rumplestiltskin."

Also: "Bhoutros Bhoutros Ghali."

It's okay to lie about certain aspects of your sexual history.

Not aspects that involve viruses or her sister.

Because the truth will out, eventually, and when it does—hoo, boy!

Contrary to persistent reportage touted on the covers of certain women's magazines, there are no "new" positions.

So relax. You pretty much know them all.

There is no shame in the missionary position.

That said, exclusive deployment of the missionary: Snoresville.

The missionary position was named for spreaders of the gospel who preached that men should assume a dominant posture over women in all endeavors.

While we're tempted to say, "Spread this gospel, baby!," we shan't.

Not again, anyway.

If you're reading this, you're probably not a missionary.

Whether or not you are a missionary, you're a blame fool to eschew the carnal pleasures of the crab, the snake, and the wheelbarrow.

The crab: Man lies on his back, woman sits atop him facing away from his face; upon insertion, she leans back and looks up at the ceiling, supporting herself with her hands and feet on the floor.

The snake: Either man or woman lies on back, other lies on top, with bodies fully in contact from toes to faces, and insertion occurs with no spreading of the legs at all. Ssssssssuper.

The wheelbarrow: Man is standing; woman is on floor in front of him, her body facing down. He hoists her by the legs and hips, she lifts her torso with her arms, as if aiming to perform a handstand, and, insertion! Can be utilized to parade around the house or garden during the act.

Extra Bonus Position: The Cooper, in which you lean back dispiritedly with beads of sweat on brow, while she repeats over and over, "Don't worry, it happens to everyone—let's just cuddle."

It is crucially important that you do not have sex the same way every time.

Put another way: Having sex the same way every time makes people want to have sex with different people just to vary things.

News from the womenfolk: They would appreciate it if you would indulge their occasional desire to integrate things like bubble baths and scented candles into the making of the love.

Caveat: Sex in bathtubs is not so easy. But then nothing worth doing is.

News from the womenfolk: It is not totally inconceivable, this idea of asking her to face the wall—but you first must know her very, very, very well.

If you do not know to what the previous item refers, it is best that it stays that way.

Top 10 Worst Morning-After Exit Lines

10. Is it just me, or do you feel a burning sensation?

 9. Hey, you're not Mary Ann!

 8. Hate to go, but it's my sister Peggy Sue's due date and Momma said I'm not allowed to miss the birth of one more kid of mine.

 7. If you need to reach me, I'll be at the rectory.

 6. Grab the trash on your way out, 'kay, babe?

 5. Can you leave me a few of those condoms?

 4. Damn! Left the puppies in the dryer!

 3. So what do I owe you?

 2. You're 18, right?

 1. Whoa, that was a mistake.

Top 10 Worst Breakup Lines

10. I think we both know this isn't working out.

9. I think one of us knows this isn't working out.

8. If I've told you once, I've told you ten times: The name is Jennifer now!

7. I'm trouble, baby, with a capital T.

6. You're a real ballbuster, you know that?

5. My wife is having a bigger problem with us dating than I thought she would.

4. We'll always have Coney Island.

3. It's not you, it's me.

2. It's not me, it's you.

1. Buh-bye.

CHAPTER five:

In which your unjust reputation as a player is handily debunked, as is that of Wilt the Stilt, whether or not to be a barker, and how to bring this thing to a rollicking, if you will, climax.

The official, public version of the number of people you've slept with: half the number of people you've actually slept with.

Unless it's less than ten, in which case, say it's less than ten.

Or more than 25, in which case, you are a virgin. This is your very first time. She is to be very, very gentle.

By the way, Wilt Chamberlain was full of shit.

Average age at which people lose their virginity: 16.

Average number of sexual partners in a man's life: six.

Average number of sexual partners in a woman's life: two.

Just because she acts disinterested doesn't mean she isn't interested.

When she says she is a virgin, she is most likely a virgin.

Which is to say, one inappropriate response to such an assertion would be uncontrollable laughter.

In re virginity: It is safer to leave the boldly-going-where-no-man-has-gone-before to space explorers in skintight polyester uniforms.

Then again: You could learn from a guy like Shatner, you know.

Joke: Experienced guy says to virgin, "If you want to have sex, let me know by tugging on it once. If you don't want to have sex, tug on it 379 times."

Women talk among themselves.

This point—not a theory, by the way, but an inviolate fact—foretells great peril if you're one of those missionary-only guys mentioned in the previous chapter.

The result: a six-pack of Schlitz and a porn tape.

Always an option: gay sex!

We're not saying you should exercise it—merely that it's always an option.

Speaking of the love that once dared not speak its name but is now a staple of the best television sitcoms: Every guy needs a gay friend.

During your exertions, most women don't want you to be completely silent.

Some women, in fact, want you to curse like a sailor.

Others, when they hear you talk dirty, will find your attempt to impersonate an S&M daddy sort of ridiculous.

One wants to get a sense of the other's preference as regards dirty talking before one overdoes it.

Similarly, moaning, barking, shrieking, yelping.

Also yodeling. Because nobody, but nobody, really likes yodeling.

Do not moan, bark, shriek, yelp, or yodel louder than she does.

Extra Bonus Mental Picture: During his lifetime, chances are strong that the famous yodeler Slim Whitman may very well have participated in sex.

At your age, there's no such thing as a truthful woman who says, "Gee, I've never done this before."

She knows you're lying, too.

Now, then: Let's bring 'er in for a landing, here:

You are talking (a little), maybe.

You are listening (a lot), definitely.

If you violated the earlier maxim about yodeling, you are now yodeling no more.

You are focusing upon her sounds, her movements, her responses.

Because of this finely honed sensitivity, you are putting to practice the things you have learned— from her, from her predecessors, from this little book—with complete confidence, because they have become second nature to you.

Again: frequent fleeting touches of her arm, hand, back.

You are bearing in mind the fact that—how many times must the womenfolk tell us this?—the finale, the fireworks, they are not the only goal in sex.

You are remembering (once more, with feeling):
It's about her.

You'll know when.

Because she'll tell you.

Maybe not verbally, but she'll tell you.

And finish at the neck.

Gauge the extent to which she desires cuddling by noting whether she is, in fact, cuddling.

Do not, under any circumstances, attempt to sing the Engelbert Humperdinck number "After the Loving" at this point.

Or any other point.

And as for "Was it good for you?"—you should never have to ask.